MICKEYISMS

30 Tips for Success

The Honorable Mickey Ibarra

This book is available for purchase at Lulu.com,
Amazon.com, and BarnesandNoble.com.

ISBN: 978-1-4834-2990-8 (sc)
ISBN: 978-1-4834-2991-5 (hc)
ISBN: 978-1-4834-2992-2 (e)

Because of the dynamic nature of the Internet, any web addresses or links contained in
this book may have changed since publication and may no longer be valid. The views
expressed in this work are solely those of the author and do not necessarily reflect the
views of the publisher, and the publisher hereby disclaims any responsibility for them.

Any people depicted in stock imagery provided by Thinkstock are models,
and such images are being used for illustrative purposes only.
Certain stock imagery © Thinkstock.

Lulu Publishing Services rev. date: 5/14/2015

To the best brother in the world, David Ibarra, my colleague
and friend who first coined the term "Mickeyisms," Michelle
Minguez, and the joy of my life, my daughter, Lina Marie.

To my grandchildren, Gabriel and Lily Jane, who I hope
will benefit most from these tips for success.

CONTENTS

FOREWORD

Anyone who knows Mickey Ibarra knows he has a special talent for bringing leaders together, including many elected officials past and present. Mickey is a "uniter." I don't know anyone in politics who has done more to promote others.

In his first book, *Mickeyisms: 30 Tips for Success*, Mickey shares the most valuable lessons or "Mickeyisms" learned in his thirty-year career in Washington, DC. His desire is to simply share what he knows with others who may benefit as they strive for success. Some of the Mickeyisms are standard fare: "Dream big," and "Eighty percent of success in life is just showing up." Others are reminders that character and integrity are powerful traits in true leaders: "Always aim to be as vigorous in your praise as you are in your criticism."

One of Mickey's most valuable lessons in politics was learned while serving as director of intergovernmental affairs for President Bill Clinton: "Winning in politics is about addition and multiplication; losing is about subtraction and division." Other lessons came from challenges he encountered on his way up the ladder of success. For example, while working for President Clinton, Mickey discovered the power of "Tell 'em what you *can* do," to soften the impact of saying no when it is not possible to fully satisfy a request.

Mickey is always promoting our leaders because he understands that the role of leadership is to nurture the next generation, and that the role of leaders is to bring us together. Mickey is an incredible advocate for our community—not just the Latino community but for all communities of this great country. He is a leader among leaders, a humble man, an advocate, a true friend, and a brother. He is a man who lives by his words: "Others may try to tear us down, but we must build each other up."

—The Honorable Antonio Villaraigosa;
Mayor of Los Angeles, California, 2005–2013; Chairman of the
Democratic National Convention, 2012; Los Angeles City Council,
2003–2005; and Speaker of the California Assembly, 1998–2000.

ACKNOWLEDGMENTS

A big thank you to Maria Perez-Brown, book project manager; Steve Canning, photographer; Norma Vega, strategic partner; Roxana Olivas, Laly Rivera and the Ibarra Strategy Group team for their dedicated service.

INTRODUCTION

Only in America can a Mexican kid who grew up in Utah foster care end up a witness to history in the making while working for the president of the United States at the West Wing of the White House! It seems impossible that thirty years have gone by since starting at the National Education Association on May 29, 1984. My thirty-year career in Washington, DC has been a wonderful journey with more learning opportunities than I could have ever imagined possible: thirteen years at the NEA, nearly four years at the White House with President Bill Clinton, and thirteen more years at the Ibarra Strategy Group. I owe so many people so much for helping me along the way.

Unlike many, including my close high school friends, I have no intention of retiring any time soon. I enjoy the work, the people, the challenge, and the lifestyle the Ibarra Strategy Group makes possible. I enjoy it all too much to let it get away. However, I have made the decision to look for more opportunities to share what I know. It is my obligation to share with others who may benefit. How selfish if I simply took what I know to the grave after so many did so much to teach me in school, at work, and at play. Actually, I hope to end my career where I started it—at the top, as a teacher—sharing what I have learned.

In addition, I intend to accept more speaking invitations to share my personal story of obstacles overcome to achieve success and to build upon the tips shared in this book. A Latino leadership book co-authored with Maria Perez-Brown is underway, and a third book is planned about my life using original materials from the Mickey Ibarra Papers donated to the JW Marriott Special Collections Library at the University of Utah. So more writing, speaking, and teaching is my future.

After thirty years in Washington, it is my turn to give back. And I am starting with this little book, *Mickeyisms: 30 Tips for Success*. This is not a commercial venture. Rather, the intent is simply to share some beliefs that have made all the difference in my career. The older I get, the more urgent it seems to offer advice for others to consider. People hear me repeat these phrases so often they are known as "Mickeyisms" at my office.

I don't pretend that any of my tips are original or new. I'm not sure I have ever had an original idea, but I know a good idea when I see it—and have often turned it into success. They inspire and motivate me, and I hope they will do the same for you. I apologize in advance if anyone is not properly credited.

SMILE

Smiling is important because it sets you apart in a positive way. It helps others feel better about themselves and about being around you.

Who wants to be around a frowning face? Those are the kinds of people you want to avoid. You want to be around somebody who smiles.

A smile is contagious. Use it often and you will go far in life.

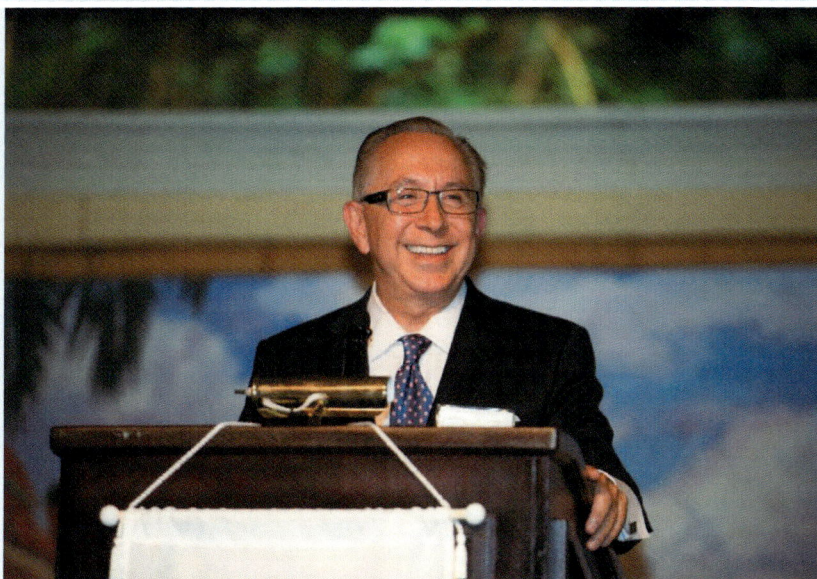

Smile often; it's contagious.

ASK

The most powerful word in the English language only has three letters: a-s-k. I'm astonished by how many people don't know this. You have to be willing to ask for what you need. You can't expect others to guess what you want. It's important to know what you are passionate about and to ask for it. Asking won't guarantee success, but it will greatly enhance your chances.

ASK is the most powerful word.

POLITICS

Politics, campaigns, and elections have been a big part of my career and my life. The most important lesson I learned from President Bill Clinton was the formula for success in politics. He explained that winning is all about adding and multiplying. Losing is all about subtracting and dividing. To win an election or to achieve success in the public arena, the goal is to reach consensus.

Good politics is about many people working together to shape policy and achieve a worthy goal in the public interest. It is where we interact to try to reach a consensus, make decisions, and make progress. That is the formula for success I subscribe to in business and in life.

Winning in politics is about addition and multiplication.

SHOW UP

Eighty percent of success in life is just showing up. That is particularly true in Washington, and—I'm sure—in other places as well. Showing up means making a commitment to people and to the causes and interests those people unite around.

I'm often told, "Mickey, you know everybody." I don't, but I'm not done yet. Showing up again and again has given me the opportunity to build relationships through a network of advocates and policymakers who have helped me earn a living and successfully promote causes I care about.

Eighty percent of success in life is just showing up.

PATIENCE PLUS PERSISTENCE

Patience plus persistence equals success—most often in equal doses. Whether you are starting a business or pursuing a personal goal, it's seldom possible to win with just one of these qualities. Patience allows you to deal with failures or setbacks without being discouraged. Persistence allows you to stay the course and not give up prematurely. The good news is that sooner or later, you *will* reach your goal.

Patience + Persistence = Success

SUCCESS

There are at least three key ingredients to achieving success: education, people, and hard work. The first ingredient is getting a good education. A good education can come in many forms—from university, community college, or professional training. My brother, David, graduated from the "college of hard knocks." He is living proof that a college degree is not always required to be successful, but you still have to master a skill, a profession, or a technology. With a good education, you get opportunities in life that others will not.

The second key is to surround yourself with good people. By surrounding yourself with good people, good things are going to happen. By surrounding yourself with bad people, bad things are going to happen. And lastly, it takes good old-fashioned hard work, which is something I have excelled at. A lot of people are smarter than me, but there are very few people who are going to work harder.

To achieve success, get a good education, surround yourself with good people, and embrace good old-fashioned hard work.

BE NICE

It's nice to be important, and it's important to be nice. That's a phrase I've embraced for a long time. It's not original, but it really worked for me when I was starting my career. I took that quote, put it on an index card, and taped it next to my phone at the White House. It's not always easy to be nice when you're being bombarded by requests from very important officials who want the president's time or the president's ear, or who want the president's views to reflect their own. While I wasn't always able to deliver the news they wanted to hear, it was always important to be nice and treat people with respect. People remember that.

It's nice to be important, and it's important to be nice.

CAN DO

One of my responsibilities as director of intergovernmental affairs for President Clinton was responding to the concerns of local and state officials, our partners in government. I had to respond to their requests for the president's assistance or for a meeting with the president or to have him speak at a public official's event.

I realized early on that I had to help these partners as best I could. So even when the answer was going to be, "No, the president can't meet with you. No, we can't go to the conference. No, we can't get you into the White House reception for the Christmas event," I had to find a way to soften the impact of the *no*. I did this by offering an alternative and telling them what we could do for them first.

Once, the mayor of one of the largest cities in America asked for a personal meeting with the president while in Washington. While we were not able to schedule the meeting, we provided him with a seat in the president's box at the Kennedy Center to hear a performance of the National Symphony Orchestra. Another time, we had to turn down a mayor's invitation to speak at a conference, but we arranged for him to shake hands with the president at another event. Always lead with the *yes*. People want to know what you can do for them—not what you can't.

To Nkuuy - Always getting me things out!
Thanks - Bill Clinton

Tell 'em what you can do.

NEVER ENOUGH

One of the hardest lessons I learned in Washington was that it is never enough to be right. I arrived at the National Education Association in 1984, believing that if you were right, others would understand, and that, of course, you would prevail on the issues you were passionate about. Well, I have been sadly disappointed. I have learned that it's never enough to be right. Life is more complicated than that. You need the right message delivered to the right people at exactly the right time with the right amount of repetition. It's never enough to be right.

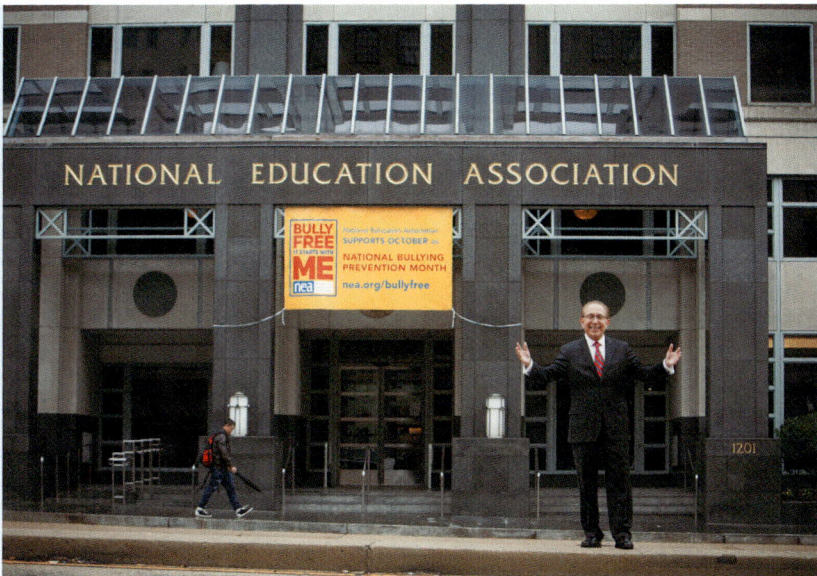

It's never enough to be right.

PRAISE

I believe it is important to be as vigorous in our praise as we are in our criticism. A person who can achieve that will be a standout in so many ways. We have a lot to criticize, and it's fair to criticize when warranted, but we also have a lot to praise. I find that many people are quick to point out what's wrong. I advise folks to look for what's right and praise it and grow it.

As a business owner or a boss, it is often necessary to give feedback or correct how a task is being completed. But it is important to understand how to balance criticism and praise. Dr. Marcial Losada, a researcher who studied this topic, explained that it is all about the ratio: you should give at least three positive comments for each negative one.

Be as vigorous in your praise as you are in your criticism.

COMMON SENSE

Throughout the years, I have learned how nonsensical so many people are in certain situations. If I could invent the common sense pill, I'd be a millionaire many times over! Common sense is the ability to call timeout, step back, and take a look at the challenges in front of you, the assets that you possess, and the relationships you have. Bring those together to come to a conclusion that's rational. Common sense is so uncommon, and those who have it are very valuable.

Common sense is so uncommon.

MISTAKES

Everyone makes mistakes, and every mistake is an opportunity to learn and improve. We all should make a commitment to get better and reduce the chances of repeating those mistakes. Most often the only tragedy of a mistake is not learning from it.

It is not always easy to understand *how* to learn from your mistakes, but there are some strategies that can help. The first is to stop seeing your mistakes as failures and instead see them as opportunities for learning. Second, be forgiving and do not blame others for your mistakes. Look at the situation as a whole to see how you could have done something differently. Would you have had a different outcome? Finally, congratulate yourself for having had the opportunity to learn something about yourself.

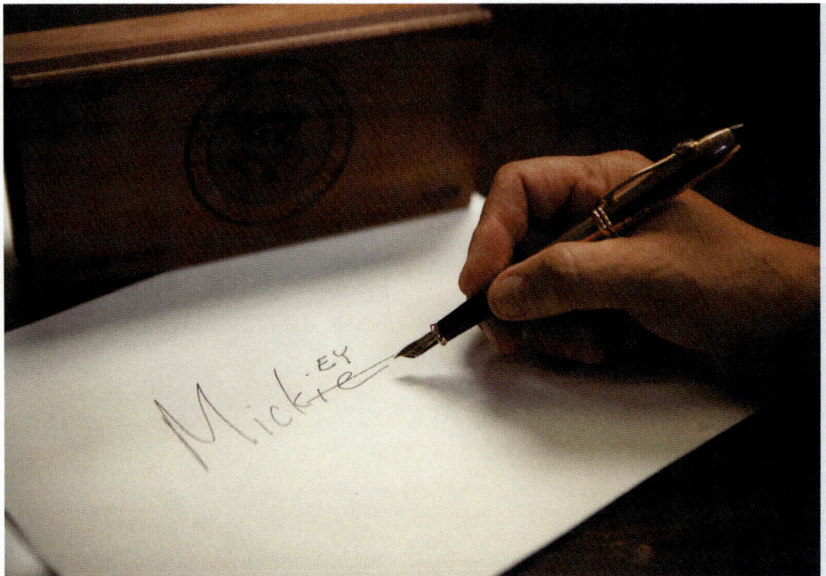

Learn from your mistakes.

GOOD LUCK

Good luck is the intersection where preparation meets opportunity. That's why it is so important to convey to young people that learning is a lifelong endeavor. It is so important for us to be prepared for opportunities that we may not even imagine possible.

As a little Mexican kid who grew up in Utah foster care, I could never have imagined that I would end up witnessing history in the making while working for the president of the United States. I will always be grateful to everyone who inspired and prepared me to seize this opportunity for public service when it came my way.

Good luck is the intersection where preparation meets opportunity.
This good luck symbol is kept in my office close to me.

BE POSITIVE

I have met so many people in my professional career who seem to be carrying the weight of the world on their shoulders all the time. Negative people wear me out, and they wear out other people around them.

Positive people see the good and praise it. They aim high and don't allow themselves to get sucked in to the negative undertow that's too often a part of our conversation. Positive people stand out, which gives them the great advantage of being more persuasive, more effective, and better human beings. I'm a positive guy. I love my life, and I want to surround myself with positive people. There are only two kinds of days for me: a good day and a better day.

There are only two kinds of days: a good day and a better day.

BUILD EACH OTHER UP

I find that too often we tear each other down rather than build each other up. This is especially true in Washington. I established the Latino Leaders Network in order to bring leaders together regardless of party affiliation or ideology. At LLN, we are dedicated to celebrating each other's successes and learning from each other's personal stories of obstacles overcome to achieve success. By listening to each other's stories, we realize that we have more commonalities than differences.

Build each other up.

RECIPROCITY

Many times, we want others to give back the effort we have made. While reciprocity may be a worthy endeavor, we also have to realize that so much of what we do in life will never fully be reciprocated. What we do can't simply be about an expectation of reciprocity. Be authentic and treat people the way you want to be treated, even though they may not reciprocate.

In situations where I'm disappointed with people, more often than not, I discovered that what goes around comes around. When people treat others poorly, are difficult to work with, or don't understand the need to give back, you don't have to do anything; just stand by because what goes around comes around.

What goes around comes around.

GIVE

My brother, David Ibarra, has built several very successful businesses and encouraged me to do the same following my tenure at the White House. He taught me that you have to give, give, give before you get, get, get.

In business and in life, it's not a quid pro quo. Sometimes you have to give a lot more than you get in return. But if you continue to give, give, give, you are going to accomplish a lot of good things—and you are going to be a better person for it. I also believe when you give, give, give, you enhance the possibility to get, get, get.

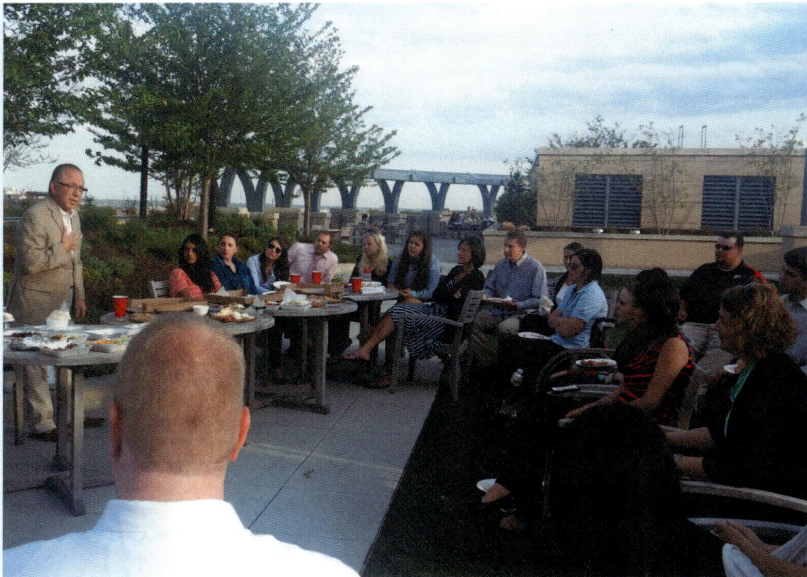

You have to give, give, give before you get, get, get!

LEADERSHIP

In my experience, leaders are those who make a difference wherever they reside, with whatever responsibilities they hold. They tend to be passionate, focused, and organized people who challenge the status quo if it is not working.

Leaders can articulate clear visions for their organizations and inspire positive changes in those who follow. They are involved in the "process" of how to do things in their organizations, and they can inspire and help every individual in their organization succeed. Leadership is about achieving success as a team.

Leadership is about achieving success as a team.

CLIENTS

I often remind those who work with me that our clients make this all possible. If our clients don't retain us to assist them, we're out of business. And there are no permanent clients. It's important to remember that our clients' problems are our opportunities to serve. So when a client comes to us with a problem, we need to be grateful and propose solutions.

One of the things I enjoy about consulting now is that I don't make many decisions. It's not my role in the executive hierarchy of a corporation. We work with many major corporations, and our job is to give them the very best advice. Once they make the decisions, we do all that we can to help them execute. When a client gets it wrong, I remind my team that they have every right to get it wrong.

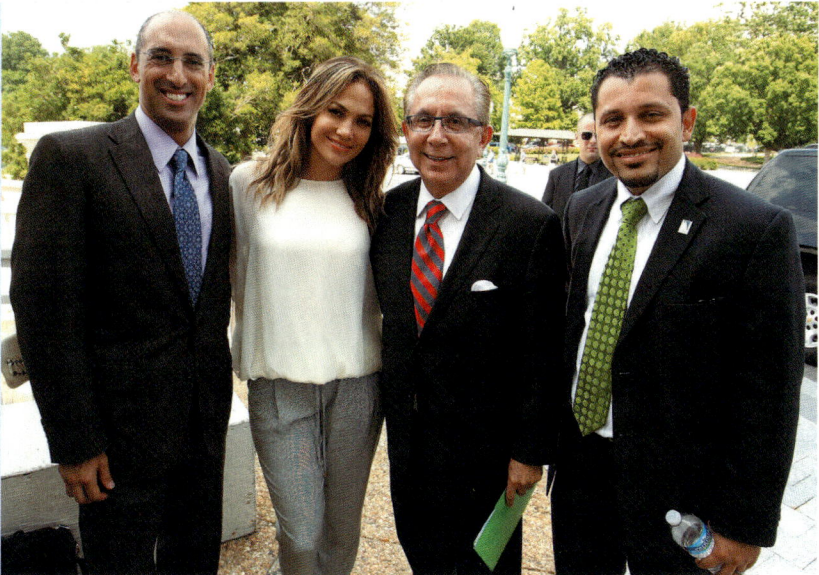

Clients have every right to be wrong.

DO IT

Do what you say! Every time you make a promise and keep it, your credibility is enhanced. Every time you make a promise and don't keep it, your credibility is reduced.

Suppose you tell your boss you'll have a presentation ready by ten o'clock the next morning. If you show up on time and give a great presentation, your boss knows he or she can depend on you. If you're late or give a sloppy presentation, you'll lose credibility.

Keeping your word is about integrity. If you do not do what you say, people lose trust and respect for you. You will be seen as someone who is unreliable. Ultimately, keeping your word is a measure of your personal integrity.

Do what you say!

COUNT IT

It is important to be able to track our progress and count our successes or our failures. When I receive a report from my employees that says, "We completed all the calls to the mayors today," I tell them that report is not helpful. How many calls were placed? How many people did we reach? How many asked for a new invitation? How many said they never saw the invitation?

I like things to be counted because when you count things, those who you work with tend to have a greater respect and appreciation for what they have accomplished. Counting is important for measuring your success. If you can't count it, you probably ought to stop doing it or start thinking about how to do it in a different way so you can demonstrate to a client that you've been delivering value for them.

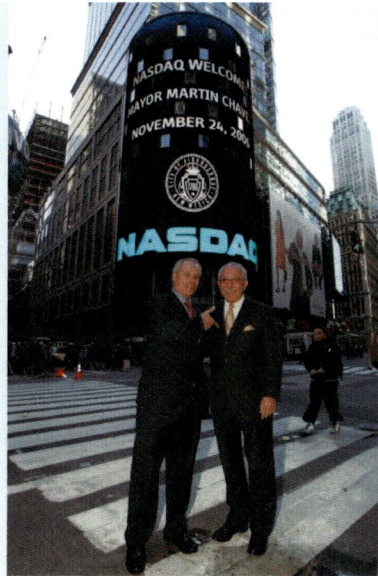

If you can't count it, you likely ought to stop doing it.

PATIENCE

Patience is an essential ingredient on the road to success. Patience is more than the ability to wait; it includes the ability to keep a good attitude while waiting.

When God was passing out patience, he shorted me some. I want things done right. I want them done now. I don't want any excuses. I had to really look at my behavior and work hard to develop patience. And I still do. I have come to appreciate that no one can make every decision or make everything right with the world. I have had to learn that sometimes there are extenuating circumstances and that life is more complicated than my timeline. It's okay to share what I expect, but it's also important for me to provide the resources for others to be successful with the requests I've made of them.

Patience is essential.

GETTING TO YES

I often talk to folks who are looking for employment, especially students who have graduated from high school, college, or graduate school but haven't been able to find that first job. Although I give them lots of advice, the most important message is that every time you get a no, you're one step closer to yes.

Omar Minaya, former general manager for the New York Mets and the first Latino general manager in Major League Baseball history, shared his story at the Latino Leaders Luncheon Series. He told us that he had applied eighteen times to be a general manager and was always told no. But he used every one of those rejections to stay focused on his goal. On the nineteenth time, he was told yes. You can get a hundred no's, and that's okay. You're just looking for one yes.

Every no is one step closer to a yes.

GOOD

For those of us who have been given so much, it is important to do good as we do well. It is our responsibility to ensure that we give back to our community, our country, and our world. I've had the privilege of joining my brother, David Ibarra, to form the Ibarra Foundation, which is dedicated to providing scholarships to Latino high school graduates who want to attend college in Utah.

Now, it's not the world, and it's not even the country—it's Utah—but that's a place where we thought we could be helpful to students like us. As young boys, David and I benefited from good people in Utah. Now we are in a position to be helpful to others who want to continue their educations. I've always said that what I want stamped on my tombstone when I'm done on this earth is: *Mickey left this world better than he found it.* That really requires doing good as you do well. Those are things that can happen together—and should.

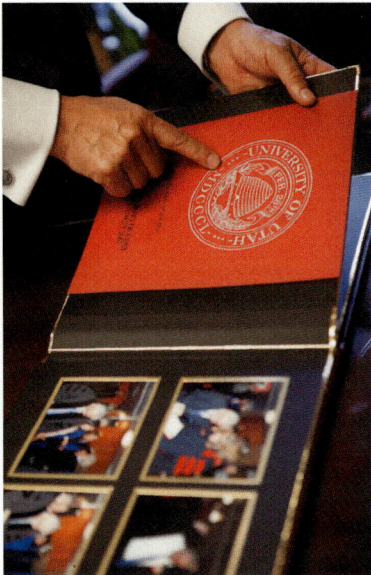

You can do well and do good at the same time and should.

LOVE

Love can be manifested in so many different ways. I love my life. I love my work. I love my family. I love the friends I surround myself with. Love is an important ingredient for a successful and happy life.

My most rewarding experience as a father has been observing my daughter embrace the values I hold dear. My daughter, Lina Marie, has given me the biggest joy in my life. I am so proud of the woman, wife, and mother she's become. My love for her is unconditional.

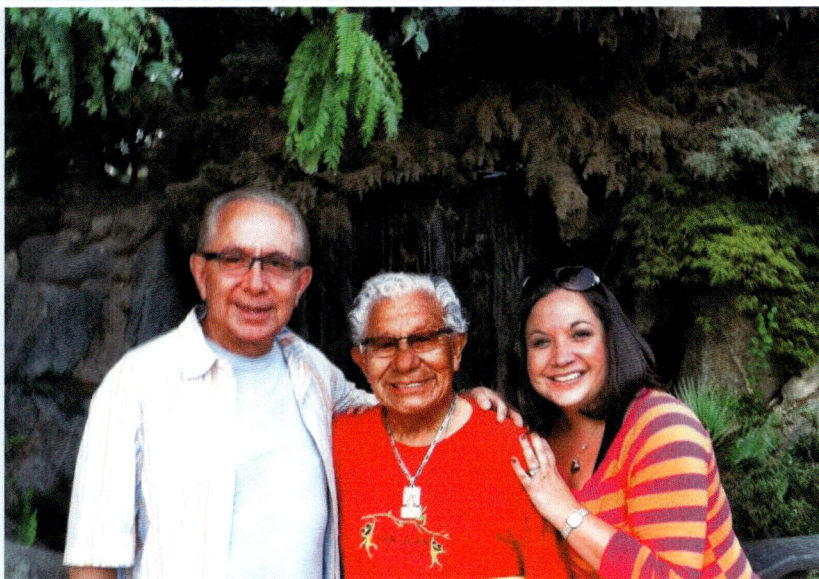

I love my life.

HAPPINESS

Happiness is one of the key words I would use to describe my life. I really enjoy helping others achieve happiness in their lives, whether it's personal or professional. I love happy clients. Oh, show me a happy client, and Mickey Ibarra is going to be happy, happy, happy. That's what we do. I'm in the happy business.

Show me a happy client, and I am happy, happy, happy.

FRIENDSHIP

I am so grateful for my many wonderful friends. My friends have enriched my life and have allowed me to continue to grow. Continue to develop friendships, pay attention to those friendships, and grow those friendships because you can't ever have too many friends.

Issues come and go; friendships should remain in place for a lifetime.

KEEP IT SIMPLE

Sometimes less is more. When you are striving for success in Washington or in life, keep it simple. I specialize in simple—complex, not so much. In fact, boiling it down to three points on each topic you are addressing with an audience is best. No one remembers more than three anyway.

Keep it simple.

PERSONAL STORY

Our personal stories are powerful, and they need to be told. It wasn't until I was in the White House that I discovered the power of my personal story. I was separated from my parents at the age of two and placed in foster care, yet here I was working for one of the most powerful people in the world. I realized the power of inspiring other people to succeed by telling my story. If it can happen to me, it can happen to you.

I created the Latino Leaders Luncheon Series as a vehicle for others to share their personal stories of obstacles overcome to achieve success.

As you discover who you are and what values matter to you, it is important to tell your story. Share the memories and experiences that shaped your life with your loved ones and others who may benefit.

Share your story with others.

DREAM BIG

It's so important for us to imagine what we want to achieve. The first thing you have to do is figure out what you really want. What are you passionate about? Many of us are reluctant to embrace our own worthiness or abilities. Many of our limitations are self-imposed. Often, nobody's placing a limit on you. You're placing limits on yourself by saying things like "I can't" or "I'm afraid." It's really important for us to dream big and release ourselves from all self-imposed limitations. Once you imagine what you want to achieve, push the limits. Make sure to dream big.

Dream big.

ABOUT THE AUTHOR

The Honorable Mickey Ibarra is president of the Ibarra Strategy Group, a government relations and public affairs firm in Washington, DC. He is the founder and chairman of Latino Leaders Network, a nonprofit organization dedicated to "bringing leaders together." Ibarra was appointed assistant to the president and director of intergovernmental affairs at the White House in 1997. He began his career as a teacher in Utah before joining the National Education Association. Ibarra is a graduate of the University of Utah, where he was awarded an honorary doctorate of humane letters in 2007.